Jesus Under the Hood

Dr. Jim Turrell

Jesus Under the Hood

ISBN: 978-0-9667986-6-1

First edition printed December 2024

Printed in the United States of America

This is a work of non-fiction. The ideas presented are those of the author alone. All references to possible results discussed in this book relate to specific past examples and are not necessarily representative of any future results specific individuals may achieve.

Dedicated to my brother Terry Turrell

Cover Art by Kevin Toft and Ted Toft

Contents

Foreword

By Paul Williams

Academy, Grammy, and Golden Globe-winning composer

Dr. Jim Turrell, my minister, has written a spiritual parable that is, in my humble opinion, a masterpiece!

Jesus Under the Hood finds Jesus and his disciples returning to earth and moving His ministry into a small town neighborhood garage in Costa Mesa, California.

Here sermons are replaced with friendly conversation as warm and welcoming as dialogue on an episode of Cheers!

In this wonderfully common, comfortable and unintimidating setting, souls are repaired alongside the vehicles that deliver them. Sweet inspiration and unexpected guidance is given freely in this very special modern day workplace.

Here, the customer and you, dear reader, will find Jesus, calmly sharing truths and changing spark plugs, Peter, leaning against a workbench, wiping his hands on an oily rag, while discussing forgiveness or the power of attraction. James, cleaning fuel lines, fishing for debris beneath the cars chassis, an apostle in stained coveralls.

Dr. T, you have given us Jesus as a close and comforting companion, as He is eternal, the healing savior!

The end result is a brief journey that effortlessly takes the wisdom of the Lord, as transcribed in Aramaic, the original language Jesus spoke, and lovingly delivers its true message. In his words are truly the keys to a kingdom! The power of love, forgiveness, and the elegance of kindness."

Anyway, Jim, I just loved it and I think it's gonna have a wonderful life expanding your ministry in ways unimagined.

Introduction

The Narrator's Journey to a New Understanding of God

I grew up immersed in traditional Christian values, part of the W.A.S.P. (White Anglo-Saxon Protestant) community. My early life was steeped in Lutheranism and Methodism, and like many, I never questioned the existence of God or the teachings of Jesus. My parents instilled in me a basic sense of Christian morality, and I experienced God in a way that made me feel safe and loved as a child. This all changed as I grew older, and I began to hear different versions of God—ones filled with fear, judgment, and punishment.

As I reached high school, I began to feel the weight of religious expectations. Suddenly, God wasn't just the loving figure I had known but a being who demanded obedience under the threat of being left behind. The comforting Christianity I had experienced felt like a shirt that didn't fit anymore, and I was left confused and disillusioned.

It wasn't until much later in life, after years of soul-searching, music, and teaching, that I found a spiritual path that resonated with me. My wife and I explored various spiritual traditions—Eastern philosophies, Christian denominations, and everything in between. Eventually, we stumbled upon Religious Science, which offered a way to connect with God that made sense to us. We kept going back every Sunday and, through classes and study, I began to realize that the God I had always believed in — one of unconditional love — never left me.

Through Religious Science, I learned that God is not a punishing deity, but an ever-present, loving force that is always available. My understanding of Jesus transformed as well. No longer did I see Him as a gatekeeper of salvation, demanding obedience and compliance. Instead, Jesus became a guide — someone who showed us our own potential, and how to live a life filled with love, forgiveness, and service.

My Beliefs About Jesus' Mission

The more I studied, the more my view of Jesus' mission evolved. I came to see Jesus not as a divine exception, but as a way-shower — someone who came to demonstrate what humanity is capable of when we align ourselves with divine love. His mission was not to judge or exclude, but to include, uplift, and remind us of our own divine nature.

Jesus' teachings point us to a way of life that goes beyond dogma and rules. Here are ten principles I've come to believe we must adhere to in order to live the life Jesus envisioned:

Love Your Enemies – Love is the highest form of expression, and Jesus taught us to extend that love even to those we perceive as enemies.

Do Not React Violently – Jesus showed that violence is not the answer; instead, He taught us to respond with peace and understanding.

Give God What Belongs to God – Jesus often pointed out that our true allegiance is to the divine within us, not to external forces.

Stop Looking for God Outside of Yourself – The divine presence is within each of us, not in distant places or doctrines.

Wake Up to Your Inner Magnificence – We are all created in God's image and are part of God's divine plan. It's time we embrace our true potential.

Once You Find Your True Self, Let Go of Everything Else – Jesus' message is one of letting go of ego and worldly attachments to discover the divine essence within.

Be of Service – True fulfillment comes from serving others and making a positive impact on the world.

Action Speaks Louder than Words – Jesus lived His message, and so must we. Our actions should reflect our beliefs.

Nothing Can Change Until You Forgive – Forgiveness is key to personal transformation. Until we forgive, we remain chained to the past.

Don't Forget the Real Nature of God – God is love, not a judge or a punisher. We must always remember this truth as we navigate life.

A New Understanding of Jesus and God

My journey led me to a more expansive understanding of both God and Jesus. I studied the works of scholars, including Dr. Rocco Errico, who specialized in Aramaic, the language Jesus spoke. His insights, along with the teachings of Dr. Ernest Holmes, founder of Religious

Science, helped me realize that much of what we've been taught about Jesus has been filtered through centuries of dogma.

I came across the book *The Five Gospels*, which details the findings of biblical scholars who used historical analysis to separate the probable words of Jesus from later interpretations. Through this study, I began to see Jesus not as a demigod with supernatural powers but as a teacher who embodied the potential of every human being. His message was universal, not exclusive to one group or belief system.

The Universal Teachings of Jesus

The Jesus I've come to know is not concerned with whether we follow every rule to the letter or belong to the "right" religion. Instead, He offers us a path—a way of living that aligns us with divine love and purpose. His teachings guide us to be compassionate, wise, and humble. They call us to awaken to our true selves, serve others, and forgive without hesitation.

In the end, the Way of Jesus isn't about exclusion or judgment. It's about embracing the divine within and living a life of love, gratitude, and peace. Jesus didn't come to create an exclusive club of believers but to show us all that we are inseparable from God's love and that no one is ever left behind. This is the truth that has shaped my life and ministry, and I hope it resonates with you as it has with me.

Jesus Under the Hood: Setting the Stage

As the narrator of *Jesus Under the Hood*, I invite you into a modern parable, where Jesus, the Master Mechanic, returns to Earth not to preach from mountaintops or temples, but to restore both cars and hearts in a small-town garage in Costa Mesa. Why Costa Mesa? Jesus didn't choose this town randomly. No, this is a place where the ordinary becomes extraordinary, where He and His loyal team of mechanics—Peter, James, and John—could quietly help people one car (and soul) at a time.

Let me tell you, these disciples are a lively bunch. Each of them brings their own unique personality to the garage. Peter? Well, he's always the first to jump under the hood, sleeves rolled up, a bit brash but full of heart. James, the practical one, is often found explaining things to customers with patient clarity, ensuring they understand every detail of the repair. And John? He's the dreamer, the one who adds a spiritual touch to even the most mundane repairs, gently reminding people of the bigger picture.

But what makes this garage truly special isn't just the mechanical work—it's the conversations. In between changing brake pads and tuning engines, Jesus and His disciples address some of the most pressing human concerns. Each repair becomes a metaphor for spiritual and emotional healing. It's not just about fixing what's under the hood; it's about helping people fix what's within their hearts.

Jesus explains to his disciples his plan to return to earth as auto mechanics. As Jesus stood with James, John, and

Peter, He spoke with a warmth that only a true teacher could convey.

"You're not returning to earth to preach sermons in temples or synagogues," He said, eyes alight with both seriousness and humor. "Instead, you're going back to serve as mechanics. This might seem like an unusual calling for disciples, but I'm giving you the task of learning to fix not just cars, but lives. As mechanics, you'll meet people exactly where they are—in the messiness of their daily struggles—and offer them a place of understanding and healing. This is the beginning of something new. The garage we're opening together will be called *Jesus Under the Hood*. It'll be a workshop for both cars and souls, a place where people can come for help, whether it's to get their vehicle running or to find peace within."

James looked intrigued but puzzled. "Why cars, Lord?" he asked.

Jesus smiled, sensing the depth of his disciple's question. "Think of a car as a metaphor for the soul," He explained. "Just as a vehicle can run smoothly or sputter in frustration, so can a person's life. Sometimes people need a tune-up, a realignment, or a complete overhaul. By helping them with something as tangible as a car, you're offering a way for them to understand the mechanics of their own lives. When they're ready, you'll guide them through the steps to take care of their inner engine—their spirit. When you've mastered these skills, each of you will open your own garage, sharing what you've learned, until thousands of places like ours are open across the world."

As the disciples listened, they began to grasp the deeper wisdom behind Jesus' plan. By focusing on practical, everyday needs, they would reach those who might never set foot in a temple. Through their work, they would embody Jesus' teachings in their interactions, one repaired engine and one healed heart at a time.

"You're not just mechanics," Jesus reminded them. "You are way-showers, teaching others that they, too, have the power to repair, restore, and drive forward in life."

This mission, so unconventional yet profoundly practical, would transform not only the people they served but also future generations of "mechanics" who would carry on the legacy of *Jesus Under the Hood*. Through it, Jesus' message of service, humility, and love would spread in a way that felt as genuine and grounded as the work they'd do every day.

Chapter 1

No One is Left Behind

Now, let's dive into our first chapter, "No One is Left Behind." Imagine it: a sunny afternoon, the sound of wrenches clinking against metal, and the soft murmur of customers discussing the strange sounds coming from their cars. Jesus and His disciples are hard at work, but the lessons they share go far beyond replacing a spark plug or aligning tires.

It was a slow afternoon at The Master's Garage, and Jesus was in the middle of explaining the finer points of carburetors to James, John, and Peter when Mrs. Garcia's minivan rolled in, coughing and sputtering like it was on its last leg. She stepped out, exasperated. "Jesus," she sighed, "I swear, no matter how much I try to keep this thing running, it just keeps letting me down! I fix one problem, and bam—another one pops up!"

Jesus chuckled and gave a knowing nod. "Mrs. Garcia, sometimes cars are like our lives, aren't they? Just when we think we've got things sorted, another little 'rattle' shows up." He looked over at Peter. "Alright, Peter, let's get under the hood. You up for it?"

Peter rolled up his sleeves with a grin. "If you say so, Boss!"

As Peter started poking around, Jesus continued, "Folks often feel like they're just left to fend for themselves when things get tough—like the world has moved on without them. It's kind of like this van. When it's out of

1

sync, every drive becomes a struggle. But we can fix that."
He paused, then recited with a twinkle in his eye, "You've
heard the story, right? About the shepherd with a hundred
sheep who goes out to find the one that wandered off?"

John chimed in, grinning, "Are you saying Mrs.
Garcia's van is the lost sheep?"

"Exactly!" Jesus laughed. "And we're going to bring it
back, smooth as ever!"

Just then, Peter found the culprit: a clogged fuel line.
"Here's the problem, Jesus. No wonder it's been
struggling—there's barely any flow!"

Jesus looked at Mrs. Garcia and nodded. "You see, just
like this fuel line, sometimes our own hearts get clogged
up too—by worries, fears, doubts. But if we just clear that
out, let love and forgiveness flow, things start running
smoothly again. No one, and no van, is ever truly left
behind."

Mrs. Garcia smiled, catching onto the message. "So, I
just need to unclog my heart a little?"

Jesus winked, "Exactly! Take it from me, Mrs. Garcia—
whether it's your van or your soul, the trick is to keep the
love flowing. A little faith, a little patience, and before you
know it, things start working just as they should."

As the disciples buttoned up the repairs, Mrs. Garcia
gave them a grateful smile. "Thanks, Jesus. I came in here
just hoping to get my van fixed, and I'm leaving with a
whole new perspective!"

Jesus grinned. "That's the magic of *Jesus Under the
Hood*—you leave with more than just a working engine."

The Secular Voice of Change

A man pulls up in his sputtering sedan, frustrated and confused. He steps out of his car, venting his frustration about how the engine keeps failing despite following all the "rules."

Peter, with his characteristic straightforwardness, laughs and says, "Ah, that's like life! You can follow every rule and still end up with a broken engine if you're not tuned to the right frequency."

Jesus wipes His hands on a rag, leaning over the hood. "It's not just about the rules, my friend," He says, smiling. "It's about growth. If you cling too tightly to tradition, you'll miss the opportunity for transformation. Your car, like your heart, needs care beyond just the manual."

The Sacred Voice of Transformation

A woman comes in next, her old truck billowing black smoke. "I feel like this truck," she sighs. "Burnt out and going nowhere." James, with his usual calm, slides out from under a car and hands her a coffee. "Life is like this truck, ma'am. Sometimes you need more than a quick fix; you need transformation."

Jesus adds, "Your heart, like this engine, is built to be renewed. You're not broken; you're simply ready for new parts. Old thoughts that no longer serve you can be replaced, just like these worn-out parts. You are never junk in God's eyes."

The disciples share a smile—James' pragmatic style and John's spiritual touch complement each other without effort. Each repair becomes more than just mechanical; it becomes sacred.

The Voice of Tradition

Next up is a young man, storming in with his brand-new car that's already broken down. "How can something this new already fail?" he demands.

Peter chuckles from across the garage. "A brand-new car doesn't mean perfect," he says, tapping a wrench against his palm. "Even new things can break if the foundation isn't solid."

Jesus nods, wiping the grease from His hands. "Tradition can be like this car. You can follow the rules to the letter and still find yourself lost if you're not grounded in love and understanding. It's not about sticking rigidly to the manual; it's about learning to feel the engine of your heart and soul."

The Voice of Love

An older man, clearly anxious, pulls into the shop, worried about his brakes. "I'm afraid I won't be able to stop in time," he confesses.

John, ever the compassionate one, steps forward with a gentle smile. "Fear is like faulty brakes—it stops you from moving forward in life."

Jesus places a hand on the man's shoulder. "Love is the answer, not fear. Just like we'll fix your brakes and help you move safely forward, love will guide you past your anxieties, no matter what challenges lie ahead."

The Voice of Self-Absorption and Expectation Versus Expectancy

As the day progresses, a luxury car pulls in. Its owner, angry and self-righteous, complains that the car isn't as fast as advertised. "I paid for the best!" he shouts.

James exchanges a knowing look with Peter. "Ah, the voice of self-absorption," Peter mutters under his breath.

Jesus walks over, calm as always. "Sometimes we expect the world to give us exactly what we want, but life, like this car, doesn't work that way. It's about aligning with what we need for growth, not just what we desire."

John steps in, always ready to offer wisdom. "Living in expectancy, not expectation, will bring you peace. Life's about tuning the engine to the right vibrations, not demanding the perfect outcome."

With a wink, Peter adds, "Besides, who ever said fast was best? Sometimes life is about enjoying the ride."

And there you have it—*Jesus Under the Hood*, where cars and souls alike are repaired with love, wisdom, and a bit of elbow grease. The disciples, each with their own quirks, bring humor and heart to their interactions, reminding us all that no one is ever truly left behind. As the garage closes for the day, the message is clear: whether it's an engine in need of repair or a heart in need of healing, Jesus and His team are there, ready to restore everything to its rightful place.

Chapter 2

Forgiveness and Gratitude—A Day of Restoration at the Shop

Narrator's Setup

It's another bright morning at the shop in Costa Mesa, and as usual, the place is buzzing with life. Jesus and His disciples—Peter, James, and John—are already deep into their work. The scent of motor oil mixes with the faint smell of coffee, and the familiar sounds of ratchets turning fill the air. But today, there's something deeper going on beneath the clanks of the tools—something that has little to do with cars.

Forgiveness and gratitude are the themes of the day, and just as every car needs maintenance, so too do our hearts and minds. Here at the shop, it's not just engines being restored—it's people's outlooks on life. Let's get under the hood of our thoughts today and see what lessons Jesus and His crew have in store for us.

The Truth About Forgiveness

Peter, who never seems to be able to stay still, is furiously working on an old station wagon when Jesus, who is calmly working next to him, says, "Peter, people tend to think forgiveness is about letting others off the hook. But forgiveness is really about freeing yourself."

Peter, with a wrench in hand, raises an eyebrow. "Is that why I've been holding onto this rusty bolt for the last 20 minutes, then?" he quips, winking at Jesus.

James chimes in from across the shop, working under a sleek sports car, "It's the same with old anger. You think you're holding onto it to keep someone else accountable, but really, you're just getting stuck yourself."

Jesus chuckles softly and continues, "Exactly. The Western world, especially in religion and medicine, often operates from a dominator mindset, believing that the strongest or most controlling wins. But real power comes from the ability to let go and forgive, just as I've always taught: 'Love your enemies, and don't react violently.'"

John, with his usual calm demeanor, leans against the wall, holding a cup of coffee. "Forgiveness feels unnatural because it goes against that primal instinct. It's like trying to drive a manual car when you've only ever driven an automatic. You can do it, but it takes some practice."

As the disciples laugh, Jesus adds, "Forgiveness isn't about excusing the wrong. It's about choosing not to let the wrong control your life. It's freeing your spirit, like finally fixing that old transmission and watching the car run smoothly again."

The Trained Mind

Just as a well-maintained car engine runs smoother with proper tuning, Jesus begins to explain the concept of a trained mind. He looks up from the car He's working on and says, "The untrained mind reacts — just like when a car engine misfires when it's out of sync. But the trained mind... the trained mind becomes proactive, like an engine that's been tuned just right."

Peter nods while tightening a bolt, "Yeah, when you've got a trained mind, you're not jumping at every noise your car makes. You know what to focus on, what needs attention, and what's just part of the ride."

Jesus steps back, wiping His hands on a rag. "Life's energy — just like the fuel in these cars — is always present, always ready. But it's the way we direct that energy that makes all the difference. A trained mind can see beyond what's right in front of it. It doesn't just react to circumstances, but it creates opportunities, focusing on what truly matters."

James, who's always practical, adds, "It's like knowing when to take your car in for a tune-up, not because something's wrong, but because you know that regular maintenance keeps things running smoothly. That's the trained mind. It prevents breakdowns before they happen."

Jesus nods in agreement. "Exactly. When your mind is trained, it doesn't get stuck in the same loops, reacting to the same problems. It knows how to keep moving forward."

Gratitude and Generosity

Just as the team is finishing up with one of the cars, John takes a moment to wipe his brow. "Gratitude is like the oil that keeps everything moving smoothly. Without it, everything just grinds to a halt."

Peter, who's now leaning against a toolbox, says, "And it's funny. People don't think about oil until it runs out. Same with gratitude. They don't realize how important it is until they're running on empty."

Jesus nods, "Gratitude is powerful because it aligns you with the flow of the universe. It opens up the doorway to receiving more. Like I said, 'Trust that you will receive everything you pray and ask for, and that's the way it will turn out."

James, adjusting the side mirror of a car, grins, "And the beauty of it is, gratitude doesn't just help you — it helps everyone around you. It's like spreading good fuel in a gas tank. When you're grateful, you're generous with your time, your energy, your love. You stop thinking about what you lack and start giving from what you have."

Jesus smiles at James, adding, "That's because a generous spirit doesn't run out. It's like a well-tuned engine; the more you use it, the better it runs."

The Trained Mind vs. The Untrained Mind

The conversation shifts as the sun begins to dip lower in the sky, casting a golden glow over the shop. Jesus turns to Peter, who's fiddling with a stubborn spark plug, and says, "Peter, the untrained mind is like this car before you fixed the engine. It reacts wildly, without control, going wherever the road bumps take it."

Peter, now covered in grease but grinning, says, "Yeah, but with a trained mind, you're the one in the driver's seat. You're steering, not just reacting to the bumps in the road."

Jesus continues, "The untrained mind fears, blames, and holds onto guilt. But the trained mind, well... it sees fear for what it is—False Evidence Appearing Real. It doesn't let the bumps in life dictate the journey. Instead, it gives thanks for each lesson, and forgiveness for each mistake."

John, still nursing his coffee, adds, "And when the mind is trained, it's prepared. Like fertile soil waiting for seeds to grow, it's ready for the goodness that life wants to give."

James chimes in, "But the untrained mind—it's like driving without oil. Everything starts to seize up. It can't see the blessings, just the problems. It's focused on what it doesn't have, instead of what it's been given."

Jesus smiles as He finishes His work on the car. "When you train your mind with gratitude and forgiveness, you stop living reactively. You begin to live proactively, creating the life you want, not just enduring the one you have."

The Doorway

As the day comes to a close and the shop prepares to shut its doors, Jesus wipes His hands clean and looks around at His disciples. "The door to a better life is always open. The only question is, are you willing to walk through it?"

Peter, always the one to lighten the mood, throws a towel over his shoulder and says, "Well, if the door's as rusty as some of these car doors, people might just need a little WD-40 to get it open!"

John laughs, "Yeah, and forgiveness and gratitude? Those are the WD-40. They're the key to getting that door unstuck."

Jesus chuckles, "Exactly, Peter. The world makes you believe that the door is locked, but it's not. You just need to unlock it with forgiveness and gratitude. The trained mind knows this. It doesn't rely on the opinions of others or the reports of the world. It trusts in the principles that are as universal as gravity."

As the disciples clean up the shop, Jesus looks up at the setting sun and quietly says, "Remember, the door to a better life isn't found outside of you. It's within. And the only way to open it is through forgiveness and gratitude."

The shop may be closing for the night, but the lessons continue to reverberate long after. Just like the cars that leave the garage in better condition, so too do the minds and hearts of those who enter this sacred space.

And with that, the day ends at *Jesus Under the Hood*, where every repair is an opportunity to grow, heal, and transform—not just the car, but the soul.

The Parable of the Workers in the Workshop

As the sun began to dip behind the hills, casting a golden light over the shop, Jesus gathered His disciples and a few of the customers who had stayed behind for the day's teachings. Everyone sat around in a loose circle — some perched on toolboxes, others leaning against the cars they had brought in for repairs. The air was thick with the scent of oil and the quiet buzz of reflection.

Seeing that it was time for a story, Jesus began, "Let me tell you about a workshop and its workers."

The disciples perked up, always eager to hear one of Jesus' parables, knowing it would reveal something profound, even if it started with something as simple as a shop.

"There was once a mechanic," Jesus said, "who owned a small but busy workshop. Each day, he hired workers to help him repair the many cars that came through the door. One morning, he went to the marketplace at dawn to hire the first set of workers. He agreed to pay them a fair day's wage and sent them to the shop to begin their work."

The disciples and customers nodded, already imagining the familiar scene of bustling mechanics, hard at work.

"A few hours later, around mid-morning, the mechanic saw that more help was needed, so he went back to the marketplace to hire more workers. He said to them, 'Join me in the shop, and I'll pay you what is right.' They agreed and joined the others."

Jesus continued, "Around noon, and again in the afternoon, the mechanic did the same — going back to the marketplace and hiring more workers. And finally, with just one hour left in the workday, he found a few more workers who had been standing idle all day. He asked them, 'Why have you been standing here all day doing nothing?' They replied, 'No one has hired us.' So the mechanic said, 'Come, work in my shop, and I'll pay you what's fair.'"

Peter, who was polishing a wrench absentmindedly, muttered, "I bet those last guys didn't expect much for just one hour of work."

Jesus smiled, hearing Peter's remark. "When evening came, the mechanic gathered all the workers to pay them. He started with those who had only worked for an hour and gave them the full day's wage—the same as those who had been working since dawn."

A murmur went through the group. James furrowed his brow. "Wait, the same pay for less work?" he asked.

Jesus nodded. "Exactly. When the workers who had been there since dawn saw this, they expected to be paid more. But when they received the same wage as the others, they began to grumble. 'This isn't fair! We've worked through the heat of the day, and yet you pay us the same as those who barely worked an hour.'"

Peter crossed his arms, clearly siding with the workers who had put in more time. "I'd be upset too, Jesus. It doesn't seem right."

Jesus chuckled softly. "Ah, but listen to what the mechanic said. He replied, 'Friends, I'm not being unfair to you. Didn't you agree to work for this wage? Take your pay and go. I choose to give the one who was hired last the same as I give you. Don't I have the right to do what I want with my own money? Or are you envious because I am generous?'"

The workshop grew quiet as the weight of the parable settled over them.

Jesus looked around at His disciples and the customers, making sure everyone was listening closely. "This," He said, "is the way of forgiveness and gratitude. You see, the mechanic's generosity wasn't about the hours worked, but about the spirit of grace. Just like in life, some people come to understanding and healing early, and some come late. But in the kingdom of heaven, there's no such thing as being too late. Everyone is given the same opportunity for grace, no matter when they arrive."

John, always the thoughtful one, spoke up. "So, it's not about the work we do, but about the gratitude we have for what we've been given?"

Jesus smiled at him. "Exactly, John. Gratitude opens the door to abundance. It allows you to receive freely, without comparing yourself to others. Those who grumbled about the wage missed the point—they had agreed to the work and the reward. But their envy, their need for more, clouded their ability to be grateful for what they had already received."

James, scratching his head, asked, "And the lesson on forgiveness? How does that fit in?"

Jesus leaned against one of the cars, looking thoughtful. "Forgiveness is about letting go of the need to measure and compare. Just as the workers who were first hired felt cheated, they clung to a sense of injustice. But forgiveness releases that. It allows you to see the bigger picture—that grace is not something we earn; it's something given freely. To forgive is to free yourself from the chains of resentment, just like that rusty bolt Peter was struggling with earlier."

Peter grinned, looking at the wrench in his hand. "So I guess that means I need to let go more often, huh?"

The group laughed, and Jesus nodded. "Yes, Peter, that's exactly it. Let go, forgive, and be grateful for what you have. It's not about how long you've been working or how much you think you deserve. It's about recognizing that all of us are given the same grace, the same love, the same opportunity—no matter when we come to it."

And with that, the day at the workshop ended not just with restored cars, but with restored hearts. The workers, the disciples, and the customers left with a deeper understanding of the lessons Jesus taught—not just about fairness, but about the profound power of forgiveness and the life-changing practice of gratitude.

Welcome to the Spiritual Tune-Up

It's not every day you get a chance to have both your car and your spirit tuned up in the same visit. But today at *Jesus Under the Hood*, the team has invited their regulars back for something special—a spiritual check-in with Jesus Himself. Sure, the garage is known for fixing engines, transmissions, and the occasional muffler, but today, it's been transformed into a sanctuary for deeper repair—the kind that gets to the heart and soul. Jesus, Peter, James, and John are on hand, not with wrenches in hand (well, maybe a few wrenches), but with wisdom, humor, and a few parables that are guaranteed to leave a lasting impact.

Jesus has been hearing from many who feel that His original message has been distorted over the years—misunderstood, misapplied, or even missed altogether. So, in true Master Mechanic fashion, He's decided to offer a tune-up. But this isn't just about adjusting your spiritual alignment; it's an opportunity to get your faith, mindset, and life back on track—just like an engine running smoothly after a tune-up.

The shop is buzzing with anticipation. As the customers take their seats, the disciples exchange knowing smiles, ready to assist their Teacher in more ways than one. Some are skeptical, some curious, but all are here to learn—about the Way of Jesus and how His teachings apply to their lives in new and profound ways.

This isn't just a gathering to talk about Scripture. Today's session is about practical spirituality. It's about getting under the hood of life's struggles and showing people how to live in tune with love, forgiveness, faith, and balance. And much like fixing a car, it starts with diagnosing the problem, clearing out the old debris, and installing new habits of thought that keep everything running smoothly.

Chapter 3
The Spiritual Tune-Up:
The Way of Jesus

Narrator's Setup

Today is a special day at *Jesus Under the Hood*. Jesus and His team—Peter, James, and John—are not just repairing cars. They've invited customers back for a unique offering: a brief spiritual tune-up. The aim? To correct some of the misunderstandings about Jesus' teachings and provide a clearer understanding of *The Way of Jesus*. The shop has been transformed into a space not only for mechanical restoration but for spiritual renewal.

As the sun rises over Costa Mesa, customers trickle back in—curious, eager, and open to the lessons the Master Mechanic has to offer. Everyone gathers around the shop, sitting on stools, car bumpers, and tool benches. The smell of grease and oil lingers in the air, but so does something more—a sense of anticipation.

The Stories, Wisdom, and Sayings of Jesus

The morning begins as Jesus clears His throat, the shop quieting in response. "Today, I want to talk about what I really meant when I shared some of my teachings— teachings that have sometimes been twisted, misunderstood, or misused. We're here to fix more than cars; we're here to fix souls."

Peter is already nodding, wiping his hands on a rag, ready to jump in. "It's like when a car keeps pulling to one side because the tires are misaligned. People's minds can get misaligned too. That's what happens when they misinterpret what Jesus taught."

James chuckles. "Yeah, and just like we balance the wheels on these cars, we're here to help you balance your life—spiritually, mentally, and emotionally."

Jesus smiles. "Exactly. So, let's start with the basics. You've heard me say, '*Have trust in God. I swear to you, those who say to this mountain, 'Up with you and into the sea!' and do not waver in their conviction, but trust that what they say will happen, that's the way it will be.*' (Mark 11:22-25)."

A hand goes up from one of the customers, a middle-aged man with grease-streaked jeans. "Jesus, I've always wondered—what did you mean by that? Can we really move mountains?"

Jesus nods. "Yes, but it's not about the physical mountain. It's about the obstacles in your life. The mountains in your mind—the doubts, fears, and worries that keep you from realizing your potential. When you have trust in the divine, those obstacles lose their power over you."

John, leaning against a tool chest, chimes in. "It's like when an engine's clogged up. You need faith—like good fuel—to clean out those blockages so everything runs smoothly again."

Jesus continues, "That's right, John. Faith isn't just believing blindly. It's about knowing that you have the power within you, through God, to overcome any challenge. But there's a catch—there's always forgiveness. *'When you stand up to pray, if you are holding anything against anyone, forgive them, so your Father in heaven may forgive your misdeeds.'* (Mark 11:25). Forgiveness opens the door to healing."

To Ask is Power

One of the customers, a woman in her early thirties, raises her hand, looking uncertain. "I've been praying for things, asking for help. But it feels like nothing is happening. What am I doing wrong?"

Jesus steps forward, placing a gentle hand on her shoulder. "You're not doing anything wrong. But sometimes, we ask without truly believing that we'll receive. Asking is power because it puts you in direct communication with the divine. *'Rest assured: everyone who asks receives; everyone who seeks finds; and for the one who knocks, it is opened.'* (Matthew 7:9-11). The key is trust and patience."

Peter, always one for a good metaphor, grins. "It's like when someone comes in here with their car sputtering. They ask us to fix it, but if they don't trust the process, they'll just keep worrying. It's not about worrying—it's about trusting that the work is being done, even if they can't see it right away."

James, adjusting the carburetor of a nearby engine, adds, "And just like tuning an engine takes time, so does spiritual growth. You've got to trust that things are aligning, even if it's not immediate. It's a process."

John, sipping on his coffee, says, "And don't forget, sometimes you have to clear out the old stuff—like old oil and filters. Same goes for your mind. You have to forgive, let go of the past, before you can fully receive."

The Way of Jesus for Intellectual, Mental, Physical, and Spiritual Life

Jesus takes a deep breath, sensing the weight of the moment. "My teachings were never meant to just serve one part of your life—they're meant to serve every part: intellectual, mental, physical, and spiritual. You have to live in balance."

Peter jumps in, "Take your mind, for example. I've seen so many people clog their thoughts with fear and doubt. That's like putting the wrong fuel in your car. You can't run on that."

Jesus adds, "Yes, and mentally, it's important to train your mind to focus on what's good, what's true. *'This sower went out to sow...some seed fell along the path...other seed fell on rocky ground...'* (Matthew 13:3-9). Your mind is like that soil. If you let your thoughts fall on rocky ground or among thorns—negative thinking—they'll never grow. But if you plant your thoughts in fertile soil—faith, trust, love—they'll flourish."

James nods in agreement. "And physically, you've got to take care of your body, just like your car. If you neglect it, it's going to break down. But more than that, your physical actions need to align with what you want spiritually."

Jesus adds, "Exactly, James. And spiritually—well, that's the core of everything. *'For the kingdom of God is within you.'* (Luke 17:21). When you take care of your spiritual life, everything else aligns."

The Disciples' Questions

As the lesson draws to a close, Peter asks, "But Jesus, what about those who don't believe? How do your teachings help them?"

Jesus, with His characteristic calm, answers, "My teachings aren't just for those who already believe. They're for everyone—those seeking truth, those lost in confusion. It's about showing the way to live in harmony with the divine, whether or not they call it faith. It's about living in love, forgiveness, and trust."

John, ever the philosopher, asks, "So how do we explain that to people? How do we get them to see?"

Jesus smiles. "By example, John. Live the teachings. Let your light shine, and people will see it. *'No one lights a lamp and puts it under a basket.'* (Matthew 5:15). Be the light, and others will follow."

Closing the Tune-Up

As the customers begin to disperse, Jesus turns to the group with a final thought. "Remember, every day is an opportunity for a tune-up—spiritually, mentally, physically. You don't have to wait until things break down. Keep your mind trained, your heart open, and your soul aligned with love. The Way of Jesus is a path of constant growth, and no one—no one—is ever left behind."

And with that, another day at *Jesus Under the Hood* wraps up, but the lessons learned will resonate far beyond the walls of the garage. For those who gathered here today, their minds are tuned, their hearts lighter, and their spirits renewed—ready to drive forward into the world with a newfound understanding of the Way of Jesus.

A New Parable: The Engine and the Driver

As the gathering settled, Jesus stood up with a gentle smile and said, "Let me tell you a story."

The disciples exchanged glances, knowing that whenever Jesus started with a story, something meaningful was about to unfold.

"There was once a driver who owned a beautiful car. The car was new, shiny, and full of potential. The driver took great pride in the car, but over time, he became distracted by the things around him. He forgot to maintain the car, neglecting to change the oil, check the tires, or listen to the subtle noises the engine made. Instead, he drove faster, demanding more and more from the car, believing it would run perfectly no matter what. After all, it had been brand new once.

One day, as he was driving down a steep hill, the car's engine sputtered, and the brakes failed. Panicked, the driver tried to stop, but nothing worked. The car eventually came to a screeching halt, not because the driver fixed it, but because it crashed into a ditch. The once-beautiful car was now dented and damaged.

Frustrated, the driver climbed out and shouted at the car, 'Why did you fail me? You were supposed to keep going, to never break down!' He kicked the bumper in anger.

Just then, a mechanic happened to pass by and asked, 'What's the matter?'

'This car betrayed me,' the driver grumbled. 'It failed when I needed it most.'

The mechanic looked under the hood and smiled kindly. 'It's not the car that failed you. It's you who failed the car. You didn't listen to the signs it gave you. You didn't care for it, and now, it's asking you to slow down, to reflect, and to make repairs. Every engine needs a tune-up. You cannot drive forever without taking care of the vehicle that carries you.'

The driver, realizing his mistake, hung his head. 'I didn't know. I thought it could run on its own, without me paying attention.'

The mechanic nodded. 'That's how life is. If you don't nurture your heart, mind, and soul, the engine of your life will eventually sputter and stall. But the good news is, it's never too late for a tune-up. If you're willing to stop and make the repairs, the car—and your life—can be restored.'"

Jesus paused, allowing the parable to sink in, and then said, "The car is like your soul, and the driver is you. Your spiritual life, your heart, and your mind—if you neglect them, they too will break down. But if you take care, if you listen to the signs, and trust in the process of repair, you'll find that no matter how far you've gone off course, there's always a way back."

Peter grinned, jumping in with his usual enthusiasm. "It's just like when someone brings their car to us and says, 'I haven't changed the oil in two years, but I don't know why it's not running!' You can't just expect everything to work perfectly if you ignore the basics."

James, always the practical one, added, "And it's not just about fixing it once and forgetting it. It's about regular maintenance—checking in with yourself, with your spiritual health, with your relationships. That's how you keep everything running smoothly."

John, still leaning against the tool chest, nodded thoughtfully. "Just like in the story, when you drive yourself too hard without paying attention, it's not the car that betrays you—it's you who betrays the car. The same goes for life."

Jesus smiled at His disciples' insights and then turned back to the group. "So, remember, it's not just about the times you break down. It's about how you care for your soul, your mind, and your body along the way. Don't wait until you crash into a ditch. Regularly take the time to tune up your life, forgive the dents and mistakes, and keep moving forward in love and faith."

The crowd murmured in agreement, the parable resonating deeply. Jesus, with His calming presence, closed with a simple reminder: "No matter how damaged you feel, no one is beyond repair. The key is to listen, to trust, and to care for the life you've been given. The journey is not just about the destination—it's about how you travel."

With that, the customers and disciples alike sat in quiet contemplation, reflecting on the spiritual tune-ups they each needed, both for their cars and for their lives.

Chapter 4

Jesus and the Ten Cause and Effect Lessons of Customer Support

A Day in the Shop

Narrator's Setup

It was another busy day at Jesus Under the Hood. The shop hummed with the sounds of ratchets turning, engines revving, and the occasional clatter of tools hitting the floor. As usual, Jesus and his disciples—Peter, James, and John—were deep into their work. But today, the lesson wasn't just about fixing cars. Today, Jesus was ready to share profound wisdom on customer support through the lens of auto repair, connecting each teaching with lessons for dealing with customers effectively.

As they worked, Jesus began sharing his insights with his disciples, weaving together the world of mechanical repair and the deeper spiritual lessons of customer care.

Lesson 1: Love Your Enemies (Love Difficult Customers)

Jesus: "Peter, when a customer comes in angry and frustrated, they're like a car with an engine knocking. It feels like they're attacking us, but really, they're just in need of some fine-tuning. Remember what I said: 'Love your enemies and pray for your persecutors.' In customer support, that means loving your most difficult customers."

Peter: "But Jesus, some of them are downright rude. How can we show love to someone who's treating us badly?"

Jesus: "Think of it like this: when a car keeps breaking down, we don't hate the car. We fix it. Approach the customer the same way. When you show them kindness, even when they're upset, their frustration melts away. They'll see that you're there to help, not to fight."

Lesson 2: Don't React Violently (Stay Calm in the Face of Hostility)

James: "What about when a customer starts yelling, Jesus? It's hard not to react."

Jesus: (*smiling*) "Ah, James, that's when we turn the other cheek. Don't react violently, whether in word or thought. Respond with calmness, like how you carefully replace a worn-out brake pad instead of slamming the door shut."

John: "So, if a customer sends a nasty email, we don't snap back?"

Jesus: "Exactly. You respond with patience and an open mind. Like handling a car's sensitive wiring, you deal with their concerns carefully. Soon enough, their anger will shift, and you'll find a solution without escalating the issue."

Lesson 3: Give What Belongs to the World (Recognize What's In Your Control)

Peter: "What about things we can't control, like shipping delays or parts being out of stock?"

Jesus: "Give the emperor what belongs to the emperor; give God what belongs to God. Some things are beyond your control, but there's always something within your power. When a car part doesn't arrive on time, you can't change that. But you can control how you communicate with the customer, offering solutions or compensations."

James: "So, we acknowledge the issue, but don't dwell on what we can't fix?"

Jesus: "Exactly. Be honest about what's out of your hands, but always focus on the solution you can provide."

Lesson 4: Stop Looking Outside for the Solution (The Solution Lies Within)

John: "Sometimes we get stuck looking for complex fixes when the answer might be simple. How do we avoid over-complicating things?"

Jesus: "The Father's rule is spread out upon the earth, but people don't see it. In customer service, the solution often lies within your own system. Many customer issues can be resolved by reviewing internal processes—like using the right oil to prevent an engine from seizing."

Peter: "So, instead of outsourcing or blaming external factors, we look within our own operations?"

Jesus: "Yes. Often, the tools you need are already in your hands. Don't overcomplicate things."

Lesson 5: Wake Up to Your Inner Magnificence (Recognize the Power of Small Gestures)

James: "What about those small gestures, Jesus? Do they really make a difference?"

Jesus: "Just as a small bit of leaven causes bread to rise, a small gesture in customer service can have a big impact. Sending a thank-you note after fixing a customer's issue can turn an average interaction into a memorable one."

John: "Like remembering their name, or following up after a repair?"

Jesus: "Exactly. It's the little things that make the biggest difference, just like a drop of oil can keep an engine running smoothly."

Lesson 6: Let Go of Everything but the Core (Focus on What Matters to the Customer)

Peter: "Sometimes it feels like we get bogged down in procedures and paperwork. How do we cut through all that to help the customer?"

Jesus: "When you find a treasure in a field, you sell everything else and buy that field. Focus on what truly matters—resolving the customer's core issue. It's like tuning a car. You don't worry about the paint job when the engine needs fixing."

James: "So, we get to the heart of the problem first?"

Jesus: "Yes. Simplify the process and focus on what the customer really needs. Everything else can wait."

Lesson 7: Be of Service (Go Above and Beyond)

John: "What about going the extra mile?"

Jesus: "Remember the Good Samaritan? He didn't just patch up the wounded man; he made sure the man was fully cared for. In customer support, this means going beyond the immediate fix. Follow up, ensure the customer is satisfied, and offer more if needed."

Peter: "Like offering a discount on future services after a big repair?"

Jesus: "Exactly. When you go beyond expectations, you create loyalty, just as the Samaritan's care created trust."

Lesson 8: Action Speaks Louder Than Words (Your Actions Define Your Support)

James: "But what about customers who don't believe us when we say we'll fix things?"

Jesus: "You'll know them by what they produce. It's not enough to say you care; you must show it through action. When you promise to fix something, follow through. If you say you'll call back in an hour, make sure you do. Actions are louder than promises."

John: "So, reliability builds trust?"

Jesus: "Yes. A well-oiled engine runs smoothly because it's cared for. Your actions are the oil that keeps your relationships with customers running."

Lesson 9: Nothing Can Change Until You Forgive (Let Go of Past Grievances)

Peter: "What if a customer has been a pain in the past? Should we treat them differently?"

Jesus: "Forgive, and you'll be forgiven. Each interaction should be treated like it's brand new. Don't hold onto past grievances. It's like working on an old car — you don't dwell on the previous repairs, you focus on what it needs now."

James: "So, we wipe the slate clean?"

Jesus: "Exactly. Every new interaction is an opportunity to build a better relationship."

Lesson 10: Remember the Power of Small Gestures (Small Gestures Have Big Impact)

John: "Does every little thing really matter that much, Jesus?"

Jesus: "It's like a mustard seed. It may be small, but when it falls on prepared soil, it grows into something much bigger. A small gesture, like remembering a customer's preferences, can grow into long-lasting loyalty. Even a simple follow-up email can make a customer feel valued."

Peter: "Like when we remember a returning customer's favorite coffee?"

Jesus: "Exactly. Small acts of kindness and attention are the seeds of great customer loyalty."

Closing the Day

As the day at Jesus Under the Hood came to a close, Jesus wiped his hands clean, looked at his disciples, and said, "Remember, the key to great customer service is love, patience, and action. What we put into our interactions with customers will determine what we get back. Treat each customer with the care you'd give a prized car, and you'll see your relationships flourish."

With that, the disciples nodded in understanding, ready to apply these lessons to both cars and customers alike, knowing that the Cause and Effect principles of Jesus would guide them toward lasting success.

Chapter 5

Seven Keys to Unlocking Your Life

A Road Trip Guide with Jesus and His Disciples

It was a bright, cheerful morning, and Jesus was planning a road trip with Peter, John, and James. As they prepared the car, Jesus shared a few essential "tune-up tips" for both the journey and life itself.

"Life is a lot like a road trip," Jesus began, smiling. "You need to be prepared and make sure the car's in good shape if you want to reach your destination without too many bumps along the way. Let's go over some keys that'll keep everything running smoothly."

The disciples leaned in, eager to hear more.

One – Look Only at What You Want

"Now, imagine you're driving, but instead of looking at the road, you're staring at every pothole, rock, and detour along the way," Jesus started.

Peter laughed, "We'd be bouncing off every bump in sight!"

"Exactly," Jesus said. "In life, focus on where you want to go, not on what you want to avoid. Keep your eyes on your goals, and your path will become clearer."

He added, "Remember, 'Seek, and you will find'" (Matthew 7:7). "What you look for is what you'll see, so fix your gaze on the destination."

Quote: "The thing we look at, as well as the way we look at it, determines our destiny." — *Ernest Holmes, The Science of Mind*

Two – Never Limit Your View of Life

Jesus pointed down the open road. "Think of driving with a narrow view, like staring only through the rearview mirror. What would happen?"

John smiled, "We'd miss everything that's right in front of us."

"Exactly," Jesus nodded. "Life is full of endless possibilities, like a wide-open highway. Don't limit your view. When you open up to the full picture, your journey becomes brighter."

He added, "'If your eye is clear, your whole body will be full of light'" (Matthew 6:22). "See the opportunities, not just the obstacles."

Quote: "Do not go where the path may lead; go instead where there is no path and leave a trail." — *Ralph Waldo Emerson*

Three – Never Compromise on Fuel

"Now, let's talk fuel," Jesus continued. "What if you filled up with the wrong kind of gas?"

Peter shook his head. "That car wouldn't make it very far!"

"Right," Jesus replied. "In life, never compromise on what fuels you. Just like a car needs the right gas, you need the right energy — faith, love, and purpose."

"Remember, 'You cannot serve two masters'" (Matthew 6:24). "Don't settle for what weakens your spirit. Use the fuel that drives you toward what matters."

Quote: "To be yourself in a world that is constantly trying to make you something else is the greatest accomplishment." — *Ralph Waldo Emerson*

Four – Place No Limit on Principle

Jesus held up the car key. "This key starts the engine. Your words, like this key, can spark powerful things."

James looked intrigued. "So, you mean our words are like the ignition?"

"Exactly," Jesus said. "When you speak with faith, you start the engine of your life. Believe in what you say, and let it be the start of something great."

"'If you have faith as small as a mustard seed, you can say to this mountain, "Move," and it will move'" (Matthew 17:20). "Your words have power — use them with conviction."

Quote: "Words are molds into which life flows." — *Ernest Holmes, The Science of Mind*

Five – The Law of Attraction is a Mental Practice

Jesus leaned in, "Imagine trying to fix the car without a manual, just randomly poking around and hoping for the best."

John chuckled, "We'd be lucky to get it running at all!"

"Exactly," Jesus replied. "Life works the same way. With the right mental focus, you guide your life like a well-tuned engine. Thoughts become things, so practice steering your mind in the right direction."

"'Whoever tries to keep their life will lose it, but whoever loses their life will preserve it'" (Luke 17:33). "Let go of the worries and trust the process."

Quote: "What we are inwardly is the only thing we ever shall be outwardly." — *Henry David Thoreau*

Six – Turn Entirely from the Condition

"When a car breaks down, do you just sit there and stare at it?" Jesus asked with a grin.

Peter shook his head, "Of course not. We figure out what went wrong and fix it."

"Exactly," Jesus nodded. "In life, don't just focus on what's wrong. Look toward the solution. Shift your attention away from the breakdown to the breakthrough."

"'Do not judge by appearances, but judge with righteous judgment'" (John 7:24). "Focus on the solution, not the setback."

Quote: "There is a principle of abundance that comes to us if we look forward and trust the future." — *Ernest Holmes, The Science of Mind*

Seven – The Universe is Perfect

"Finally," Jesus said, "imagine the perfect car engine, running in perfect harmony. That's how the universe operates — already aligned and balanced."

James thought for a moment, "So, if things feel off, it might just be our perspective?"

"Exactly," Jesus said. "The universe is like a finely tuned machine. If something seems wrong, sometimes it's our perception that needs adjusting."

He added, "'A house divided against itself cannot stand'" (Mark 3:25). "Align your thoughts with life's natural harmony, and everything will start to run smoothly."

Quote: "Every particular in nature, a leaf, a drop, a crystal, a moment of time, is related to the whole, and partakes of the perfection of the whole." — *Ralph Waldo Emerson*

The disciples felt ready for the road ahead, both for the journey and for life itself. Jesus smiled, knowing they had the wisdom to stay on course.

"Remember," he said, "life is the ultimate road trip. Keep your mind clear, your heart full, and your vision wide, and enjoy the journey that unfolds before you."

With renewed purpose, they set off, confident and prepared for the adventures ahead.

Chapter 6
Jesus and the Lords Prayer

"Restoration of the Spirit: A Tune-Up for Life's Journey"

In the garage, "Jesus Under the Hood," Jesus looked up from under a vintage Mustang's hood and glanced at John, Peter, and James, who were working nearby. He wiped his hands on a rag and began speaking as they gathered around.

"Alright, guys," Jesus started, "You know how every car that comes in here has its own issues? Some need a minor tweak, others need major work. But every repair, big or small, brings the car back to what it was meant to be — a smooth, reliable ride. That's a lot like the lives of the people we meet."

John leaned on the counter, curious. "So, like, when we're dealing with people's problems, are you saying it's like getting to the root of an engine issue?"

"Exactly!" Jesus nodded. "When we pray, especially with the Lord's Prayer, it's like tuning up our own spirit. The first line, 'Our Father, which art in Heaven,' helps us remember where we come from. Like a car, if it doesn't know where it came from or what parts it needs, it won't run well. When people remember they're part of something bigger — a divine Father — they begin to see their true worth and potential."

Peter, chuckling, asked, "So, what's 'Hallowed be Thy name' then? Like a fancy way of saying we respect the Manufacturer?"

"Pretty much, Peter," Jesus grinned. "When we say 'Hallowed be Thy name,' we're acknowledging the nature of our Maker. Just like each car has a distinct purpose, each person does too. We honor that by respecting our design — our potential."

James, who loved the intricacies of wiring, looked thoughtful. "Then what about 'Thy kingdom come, Thy will be done'? What's the tune-up for that?"

"Great question, James," Jesus said, smiling. "Imagine a car with wheels misaligned. It pulls in the wrong direction, right? But when you align it, it moves true. Saying, 'Thy kingdom come, Thy will be done,' is like aligning ourselves to the path we're meant to be on. It's letting go of control and trusting the road set before us, knowing that if we stick to the right track, we're gonna get where we're supposed to be."

John tapped his forehead. "Alright, but what about our 'daily bread'? I mean, cars need gas every day, right?"

"Yes! You've got it, John," Jesus replied. "In life, we need fuel too. And we don't stock up for years at a time; we trust that each day's fuel will be there. It's the same with faith. We ask for our daily bread, trusting God to provide for each day without getting tangled in worries for tomorrow."

Peter spoke up again, scratching his head. "So, what do we do with all the junk — the mistakes? When I mess up a job here, I sometimes want to toss in the towel."

"Forgiveness, Peter," Jesus answered, looking at him kindly. "When you forgive, it's like replacing a clogged-up filter. It frees things up, allowing you to move forward. You let go of what's holding you back. And forgiving others? That's like giving them a second chance to run smoothly too."

James raised his hand playfully. "And 'Lead us not into temptation'? That's like when I'm tempted to cut corners on a repair, isn't it?"

"Absolutely, James. Every time you think of taking a shortcut that could compromise quality, remember that you're aligning yourself with integrity. Temptations are those shortcuts that promise easy results but lead to breakdowns."

The three laughed, nodding in agreement.

"Here's the bottom line, guys," Jesus said. "When we're doing this work, remember that just like we're fixing cars, we're helping people mend their lives. When a person leaves here with their car running right, they feel renewed, like anything is possible. The spirit is the same. When we align with the prayer, it's a way of doing a tune-up on ourselves so that we can go out and help others do the same."

Peter smiled, "Alright, Jesus. Guess it's time to get back to work—one tune-up at a time, right?"

"Exactly, Peter. One tune-up at a time."

As they gathered around, Jesus sprinkled a few reminders from his teachings to help his disciples and the customers see the meaning in the prayer:

Jesus glanced around, smiling gently. "Each part of this prayer speaks to something we need in our lives, just like the parts of an engine. Remember, *'I am the way, the truth, and the life.'* When we follow that truth, we get back to our original purpose—running smoothly, like we were designed to."

John, intrigued, asked, "And what about the people who come in here, feeling like they've lost their purpose?"

"Well, John," Jesus replied, "remember what I said about the mustard seed? *'If you have faith as small as a mustard seed…nothing will be impossible for you.'* Even if they feel small or broken, the prayer helps them see that they're part of something much greater. Just like a car, they just need the right repairs to find their true strength."

Peter was wiping off his hands, mulling it over. "So, when we're praying for daily bread, are we just trusting God, like you said before?"

"Exactly, Peter," Jesus replied. "And as I told the crowd, *'Do not worry about tomorrow, for tomorrow will worry about itself.'* Trust that you're given what you need each day. Don't worry about stacking up everything right now; you just need today's fuel."

James spoke up, "And forgiving each other? That's gotta be like swapping out old, rusty parts, right?"

"Right, James," Jesus said. "*'Forgive, and you will be forgiven.'* When you let go of resentment, you let go of what's clogging up the engine of your spirit. It clears the path for you to move forward. Forgiveness allows you to keep running without anything blocking your spirit."

The guys laughed, and Jesus continued, "And remember, *'Let your light shine before others.'* Each car we fix is like that. When people drive out of here, it's a reminder that even if they were once broken down, they can be restored. They can show others that it's possible to get back on the road, ready to go wherever life calls them."

Peter chuckled, saying, "Alright, Jesus. Guess it's time to get back to work—one tune-up at a time, right?"

"Exactly, Peter. *One tune-up at a time,*" Jesus said with a warm smile.

As they gathered around, Jesus decided to tell a parable, knowing it would help his disciples and the customers see the deeper meaning of the prayer and how it relates to life.

Jesus began, "Let me tell you a story. There was once a man who owned an old car. It had been with him for years, and every day, it showed more signs of age—rattling noises, worn tires, even a leaking engine. It struggled up hills and barely kept up on the highway. Soon, the man started believing his car was worthless. 'What's the point of keeping this old thing?' he thought. 'It's barely hanging on.'

"But one day, as he was about to sell it for parts, he met a wise mechanic. The mechanic said, 'This car is much more than you see. It was built with purpose, with every part carefully designed. It's meant to run, to carry you forward. But it needs some care—just a little faith in its potential. Let me work with it.'

"The man reluctantly agreed, and the mechanic worked on each part, replacing what needed replacing, cleaning out what was clogged, and carefully aligning every detail. When the man saw his car again, he was stunned. It ran better than he ever remembered. It was quiet, smooth, and strong—ready for many more journeys. The man was amazed, not only at the car but at the difference it made to feel that purpose restored.

"You see," Jesus explained, "the old car had purpose all along. It only needed a mechanic to see its value and put in the work to restore it. Just like that, when we pray, we're asking our Maker to restore us, tune us up, and align us with our purpose. When we say, 'Thy will be done,' we're saying, 'Bring me back to the life I was meant to live, even if I feel broken.' And when we trust in God's vision for us, even with faith as small as a mustard seed, we become able to go places we never thought possible.

"Like that car, even if we've been worn down by life, we're not beyond repair. We're meant to be cared for, tuned up, and renewed. And when we're aligned with our purpose, we're like that car, ready to carry ourselves and others forward on the road ahead."

The disciples and customers listened, nodding as they imagined themselves and their lives in need of that same careful restoration.

After sharing his story, Jesus looked at each of them, seeing they were ready for one last message. He took a deep breath and spoke the prayer in a way they could feel in their bones, a version they could carry with them into the 21st century:

As he finished, there was a peaceful silence. The words hung in the air, simple yet powerful, and they each felt the resonance of the prayer settling within them, like a steady hum of an engine running true.

After sharing his story, Jesus looked at each of them, seeing they were ready for one last message. He took a deep breath and spoke the prayer in a way they could feel in their bones, a version they could carry with them into the 21st century:

"Our Creator, who is with us always,
Sacred is Your name.
Let Your goodness and purpose unfold within us,
Here on earth, just as it is in Heaven.
Give us today all we need, each moment as it comes.
And forgive us for where we fall short,
As we choose to forgive others with that same grace.
Guide us away from shortcuts that lead to harm,
And protect us from what would cause us to stumble.
For this life, this strength, and this purpose
Are Yours, forever and always.
Amen."

As he finished, there was a peaceful silence. The words hung in the air, simple yet powerful, and they each felt the resonance of the prayer settling within them, like a steady hum of an engine running true.

Chapter 7

The Law of Attraction

In the auto garage *Jesus Under the Hood* in Costa Mesa, Jesus and his disciples, John, Peter, and James, were hard at work on cars with various issues. The air buzzed with the smell of oil and the sounds of tools. Jesus looked up from a vintage car and decided it was a good time for a lesson.

"Alright, guys," he called, motioning them over, "let's talk about the Law of Attraction. It's like a mystery, but it's woven into everything—just like the way we tune and repair these cars."

John, ever curious, leaned in. "A mystery, you say? How's that, Jesus?"

Jesus smiled. "Think about it this way: Life is an inner experience. What happens around us doesn't affect us nearly as much as what happens *within* us. We're like cars; the way we perform depends on what's going on inside the engine."

Peter, nodding, piped up. "So, you're saying it's not the things that happen to us, but how we respond?"

"Exactly, Peter," Jesus replied, looking thoughtful. "It's like I said in the Sermon on the Mount, *'Blessed are the pure in heart, for they shall see God.'* Our thoughts, feelings, and habits are what we see and experience in the world. To solve the mystery of life, you've got to look inside."

The Mystery

Jesus continued, "Let me tell you something interesting. Two people can look at the same car and see different things. One person might see a hopeless wreck, and the other sees potential. Why? Because they're looking at it through different memories, emotions, and ideas."

John nodded. "Like how some people keep focusing on what's wrong with their lives?"

"Exactly!" Jesus said. "*'Do not judge, or you too will be judged.'* If someone spends all their energy criticizing their problems, they just keep reinforcing them. They trap themselves in that experience. But if they look within and change their thinking, they'll start to attract new, better experiences. It's not about what happened; it's about what they *think* happened."

James raised an eyebrow. "So it's all in their heads?"

"In a way, yes," Jesus replied. "That's why I said, *'The kingdom of God is within you.'* You preserve what you hate, and you lose what you love. Whatever you focus on, you create. People who hate their jobs or relationships tend to live in a cycle of disappointment because they're trying to hold on to something they should have released."

Peter laughed, catching on. "Like someone who keeps fixing up an old beater that's clearly on its last leg?"

"Exactly!" Jesus chuckled. "When you're fixated on something that's not serving you anymore, you're not allowing yourself to move forward. Life is meant to flow and grow, not stay stagnant."

The Twinkling of an Eye

After a pause, Jesus continued, "Sometimes the right fix comes in the 'twinkling of an eye.' That's when you stop, take a breath, and let go of your worries. When you do that, you make room for clarity and peace to guide you."

John thought for a moment, looking over at a car with a warning light on the dashboard. "So, how do we do that?"

"Great question, John," Jesus replied. "To get there, you have to suspend disbelief. For a while, just *try* believing that good things are possible. Push doubt aside, even if it's just for a few weeks. Keep only the thoughts that lead you toward the life you want. It's like I said, '*Seek first the kingdom of God and His righteousness, and all these things will be added to you.*' When you focus on the good, the good finds its way to you."

Peter scratched his head, smiling. "So, kind of like when we give an old car a whole new system and, after a few test drives, it's running better than ever?"

Jesus nodded. "Yes! When you direct your thoughts to the vision of what's possible, you're creating a 'mental atmosphere' for good things to grow. If you keep your mind on lack, unhappiness, or problems, you'll attract those things. But when you focus on gratitude and hope, you start attracting more of the same. '*For where your treasure is, there your heart will be also.*'"

Where Do I Start?

James looked over at a dented car they'd been working on all morning. "So, where do we start if we want to tune up our lives like we do these cars?"

Jesus gestured to the car. "First, ask yourself, 'What are you focusing on?' If all you see are dents and dings, you're missing out on the bigger picture. Imagine what it feels like to drive a fully restored car. If you let doubt and despair creep in, say to yourself, 'You're not welcome here.' Focus only on the good you want to create."

Peter laughed, "So, if the check engine light of my mind is on, I ignore it?"

"Not quite, Peter," Jesus chuckled. "Acknowledge it, but then focus on what you want. Your life is built on what you give your attention to. If you keep looking at the negative, you're bound to see more of it. But when you focus on the blessing in front of you, good things grow."

John nodded thoughtfully. "So we're all running on the Law of Attraction, whether we know it or not."

"Exactly," Jesus agreed. "And remember, *'Ask, and it will be given to you; seek, and you will find; knock, and it will be opened to you.'* When you're clear about what you want, you're more likely to see it appear. But if your mind is cluttered with worries and complaints, you'll miss it."

Who's in Control?

James looked at Jesus, curiosity in his eyes. "So, who's really in control here?"

Jesus looked at each of them in turn. "Each of you is in control of what you choose to focus on. Nothing outside of you can change that. Once you regain control of how you think, you change your experience of the world. No one else can do that for you. *'You are the light of the world... let your light shine before others.'*"

Peter shook his head, smiling. "But it's hard, Jesus. Sometimes, it's like life's just handing you one problem after another."

Jesus put a reassuring hand on Peter's shoulder. "I know, Peter. But remember, your experience of life depends on how you choose to see it. And as long as you focus on your inner strength, you're never without hope. The Way I show you is not about correcting your mistakes; it's about changing your perspective."

Prayer is the Key to Happiness

John looked thoughtful. "So, how does prayer fit into all this?"

"Prayer is how you tune your mind to God's frequency," Jesus explained. "People sometimes see prayer as begging God to change things for them. But prayer isn't about trying to get God's attention. It's about seeing yourself as God sees you—whole, perfect, and complete."

Peter laughed. "So, no bargaining with God?"

"No bargaining," Jesus grinned. "God's not waiting to judge you. *'Your Father knows what you need before you ask Him.'* Think of prayer as aligning yourself with the good that's already here, so that you're open to receiving it."

A Simple Way to Pray

Jesus looked around at the disciples, sensing their interest. "There's a simple way to pray that can help you feel closer to God," he said. "It's about focusing on your breath and feeling God's presence with each inhale and exhale."

He demonstrated, bringing his hand in front of his heart and taking a deep breath. "Inhale slowly, then exhale, letting go of all the tension and worry. Imagine the breath as peace filling your heart. As you breathe, focus on a quality you want to bring into your life—like peace, love, or joy. Let it fill your mind until it becomes the center of your thoughts."

The disciples followed along, taking slow breaths, feeling the peace settle within them.

Be the Blessing You Want

Jesus smiled as he watched them. "Here's the last thing I'll say on this. If you want to bring something good into your life, *be* that blessing for others. Live as though you're a light, sharing peace, love, and compassion with everyone. *'Blessed are the peacemakers, for they will be called children of God.'* When you give those blessings to others, they return to you multiplied."

The disciples nodded, a sense of understanding dawning on each of their faces.

"Alright," John said, grinning, "I guess we've got some work to do—on these cars *and* on ourselves."

Jesus laughed, "Yes, John. And remember, you're always tuning up your life, just like these cars. One positive thought, one act of kindness at a time."

The garage felt lighter, as though the lessons they'd shared had filled the space with peace and purpose. And the disciples went back to work, ready to face their own lives with fresh eyes and open hearts.

Chapter 8

Stories of Love and How Love Works

Jesus Teaches John, Peter, and James about the Law of Love, with Dr. Jim Turrell's Life Lessons

~ Corinthians 1 ~

"If I speak with the languages of men and of angels, but don't have love, I have become sounding brass, or a clanging cymbal."

One afternoon, Jesus and his disciples sat beneath the shelter of a large tree. The air was still, broken only by the sound of leaves rustling in the breeze. Jesus turned to Peter, his voice calm and thoughtful.

"Peter," he began, "imagine you could speak all the languages of the world—words so perfect they could move nations. Imagine you could even speak the language of angels, so beautiful that it echoed through the heavens. But if you did not have love in your heart, your words would be empty—nothing more than noise, like the clanging of a cymbal."

Peter tilted his head, curiosity in his eyes. "So, even the most eloquent words can lose their meaning?"

Jesus smiled gently."Yes, Peter. Without love, words are hollow. True connection doesn't come from what we say—it comes from the spirit behind the words. Let me share with you a story Dr. Jim once told."

The disciples leaned in as Jesus began.

"Years ago, Dr. Jim was a teacher, passionate about his work. But over time, something began to shift. Frustration crept in, and he started to feel burned out. Each day felt heavier than the last, like walking through thick mud. His once-joyful words became tired instructions, and his heart began to close. He looked at his students not with love, but with impatience, as though they were obstacles to his peace.

"One evening, he shared his struggle with his minister. He said, 'I feel like my words are falling flat. No one is listening, and I don't know if I even care anymore.'

"The minister listened, then asked him softly, 'Jim, are you teaching with love, or are you teaching with your ego? Are you speaking to be heard, or are you speaking to serve?'

"These words hit him like a splash of cold water. That night, Dr. Jim sat in silence and prayed. He asked for his heart to be softened, for his love to return—not just for teaching, but for the students themselves. He realized he had been focused on his own need to feel respected and successful, forgetting why he had started teaching in the first place: to help others grow.

"The next day, he walked into the classroom with new eyes. He noticed the quiet student in the back, struggling to keep up. He saw the mischievous boy in the front row, not as a troublemaker, but as someone longing to be seen. His words changed—not because they were more eloquent, but because they came from a place of love. And in that love, his students began to respond. A connection returned. Teaching became meaningful again, not because he had changed his words, but because he had changed his heart."

Peter looked down at his hands, thoughtful. "So love helps us see others clearly and fills our words with purpose?"

Jesus nodded. "Yes, Peter. Love is what brings life to our words, our actions, and our relationships. Without it, we are just making noise—empty, meaningless sound. But when we let love guide us, our words carry light. They heal. They connect. They inspire."

The disciples sat quietly, letting the lesson sink in. The breeze seemed softer now, as though the world itself was listening.

As they looked out across the fields, they understood: love is the thread that ties all things together. It is the quiet power that turns noise into music, actions into blessings, and ordinary moments into something sacred.

From that day on, they spoke with greater care, not to impress or control, but to serve and connect. For they had learned that words without love are forgotten, but words spoken with love can change a life forever.

And so it is with all of us. If we let love lead, we no longer just speak—we truly *connect*.

~ Corinthians 2 ~

"If I have the gift of prophecy, and know all mysteries and all knowledge; and if I have all faith, so as to remove mountains, but don't have love, I am nothing."

One evening, as the shadows grew long and the air turned cool, Jesus sat with his disciples in quiet reflection. He turned to John and said, "John, imagine this: You could know everything—every mystery of the universe, every truth hidden from others. You could even hold a faith so great that mountains would crumble at your word. But if you do not have love, it would all mean nothing. Without love, knowledge is cold, and faith has no heart."

John furrowed his brow, turning the thought over in his mind.

Jesus smiled softly, his gaze shifting to me. "Jim, didn't you learn this lesson in the early days of your ministry?"

I nodded, the memory still fresh despite the years that had passed. "Yes, I did," I began. "There was a time when fear had a grip on me. I worried constantly about the finances of my ministry—whether we could pay the bills, whether we would survive. My prayers were full of desperation, my faith focused on fixing problems rather than trusting the path."

The disciples leaned in as I continued. "Then one day, in a moment of stillness, I realized I was missing the point. I had faith, yes, but it was wrapped in fear, not love. I was praying for outcomes instead of surrendering to God's love. So, I let go. I prayed simply: *'God, let me focus on love and service. I trust You to handle the rest.'*

"Once I shifted, everything changed. It was as though love became the anchor for my faith. My fear lost its power, and provision began to flow. Not always as I expected, but always as we needed. It taught me a truth I will never forget: faith alone can move mountains, but when that faith is rooted in love, it moves *us* — calming our fears, guiding our steps, and carrying us through challenges with peace."

Peter, who had been listening closely, asked, "So, it's not just faith that moves mountains, but faith *filled with love*?"

Jesus nodded, his voice steady and kind. "Exactly, Peter. Faith without love is like a mighty wind — it is powerful but can scatter and unsettle. But faith grounded in love is like a steady breeze that fills the sails of a ship, guiding it safely to its destination. It moves with purpose and grace."

The disciples sat quietly, letting the lesson settle deep within. They realized that faith without love becomes hollow, like an empty vessel that cannot hold water. Knowledge without love becomes sharp, like a blade without a sheath. But love — love gives everything its meaning.

In that moment, they understood that love is not separate from faith or knowledge; it is what brings them to life. Love softens, warms, and directs all that we have, making it whole.

As the evening darkened, the disciples rose with hearts full of quiet understanding. They saw, perhaps for the first time, that mountains are not always made of stone. Sometimes they are fears, doubts, and struggles we carry within. And it is love — patient, enduring, and steady — that moves those mountains, one step at a time.

~ Corinthians 3 ~

"If I give away all I have, and if I deliver up my body to be burned, but have not love, I gain nothing."

One evening, as the sun dipped below the hills and the shadows stretched long across the ground, Jesus gathered his disciples. He turned to James and said, "James, imagine a man who gives away everything he owns, even sacrifices his very life — but he does it without love. Would it matter? Would the gift hold any real value?"

James furrowed his brow and shook his head. "No, Lord. It would be empty."

Jesus smiled gently. "Exactly. Giving without love is like handing someone an empty cup. The act itself means nothing unless the heart behind it is full."

To bring the lesson to life, Jesus turned to Dr. Jim and said, "Jim, share the story of the morning you learned this truth."

Dr. Jim grinned and began, his voice warm with memory. "It happened on a simple morning not so long ago. My wife wasn't feeling well, and I volunteered to take the dogs out for their walk. At first, I'll admit, I didn't do it with love. I was frustrated, annoyed at the inconvenience, and it didn't take long for every little thing to bother me — the dogs pulling on their leashes, the cold air, the noise of the world waking up.

"But then I stopped. I could feel my heart hardening, turning the task into a burden. In that moment, I remembered that love changes everything. I chose to shift my attitude, to see this walk not as a chore but as a chance—an opportunity to show love to my wife, to care for her without complaint, and to embrace the morning for what it was: a gift.

"And do you know what happened?" Dr. Jim paused, his eyes shining. "The world looked different. I noticed the soft light of dawn breaking through the trees, the sound of the birds greeting the day, the joy of the dogs simply being alive. What began as an act of duty transformed into an act of love. The burden disappeared, and in its place was something beautiful—peace, joy, and gratitude."

Peter, who had been listening intently, smiled and said, "So, when we give without love, it's like a shadow hanging over everything we do?"

"Yes," Jesus replied, his voice calm and full of wisdom. "Without love, even the greatest gift loses its light. Love is what lifts the shadow, turning simple acts into blessings. When we give with love, our hearts expand. We pour out more than our effort—we share our spirit. Even the smallest acts, when done with love, carry the power to transform both the giver and the receiver."

The disciples sat quietly, letting the truth settle in. Around them, the evening air grew still, as though the world itself were listening. They began to understand that love is not measured by the size of the act but by the heart behind it.

Love turns the mundane into the sacred.

Love transforms duty into joy.

Love breathes life into every moment.

And so they rose, hearts open, ready to see their lives—and every small act within them—as an opportunity to give with love, knowing that in love, all things are made whole.

~ Corinthians 4 ~

"Love is patient and kind; love doesn't envy. Love doesn't brag, is not proud."

At the close of a long day, Jesus gathered the disciples closer, his presence a quiet invitation to listen with their hearts. "Now," he said, his voice steady and soft, "here is the heart of it all. Love is patient. Love is kind. Love does not envy, nor does it boast. Love does not carry pride or hold grudges. Love is humble."

Peter, always quick to respond, grinned and asked, "So, love doesn't let us puff up our chests with pride?"

Jesus smiled warmly. "Exactly, Peter. Pride makes us think we are separate, but love shows us the truth: we are one. Dr. Jim shared a time when this lesson was hard to learn."

The disciples leaned in as Jesus continued. "He once mentored a young minister, pouring his heart into her growth. He rejoiced in her success until the day she started her own ministry nearby. Some of his congregation left to join her, and Jim felt betrayed. Pride crept in, and what had been love became resentment. For months, he held onto that hurt, allowing it to cloud his heart."

John's voice broke the silence, gentle with curiosity. "Did prayer help him?"

Jesus nodded. "Yes, John. Prayer opened the door. Jim finally laid down his pride and asked for guidance. When he surrendered his hurt, love returned, like sunlight breaking through clouds. He saw himself not as the owner of anyone's journey, but as a guide, a steward of their growth. He let her go with a blessing, realizing that love never seeks to hold or possess—it gives freely, without envy or demand."

The disciples sat quietly, their hearts absorbing the weight of Jesus' words. Around them, the evening air grew still, as though creation itself paused to listen.

"Love humbles us," Jesus continued, his voice like a stream flowing over stones, gentle yet unrelenting. "It invites us to put down pride, to release comparison, and to live with kindness as our guide. Where pride divides, love unites. Where envy poisons, love heals. When we live with love, we become servants of something greater than ourselves."

For a moment, no one spoke. Each disciple felt the truth settle within them, like seeds falling into fertile soil. They looked at the world around them—the trees bending in the evening breeze, the stars just beginning to awaken, the faces of their friends—and they understood.

Love is patient when the heart aches to rush. Love is kind when the spirit longs to judge. Love does not envy another's joy, for it knows there is enough for all.

Love does not boast, for its strength lies in humility. Love lays down pride and picks up peace.

The disciples rose, their hearts stirred and ready. They carried within them a love deeper than words, greater than pride, and more lasting than any earthly accomplishment. A love patient, kind, and eternal — ready to flow into the world, just as Jesus had shown them.

~ Corinthians 5 ~

"Love doesn't behave itself inappropriately, doesn't seek its own way, is not provoked, takes no account of evil."

One day, Jesus sat with his disciples, John, James, and Peter, under the warmth of the afternoon sun. His voice carried both tenderness and wisdom as he spoke about disappointment. "A heart filled with love does not look only to its own needs, nor does it cling to past wrongs," he began. "Yet even those who walk in love can sometimes stumble into frustration."

He turned to me with a knowing smile and asked, "Jim, have you ever felt that heavy sense of disappointment?"

I nodded, recalling a lesson that had opened my heart to the deeper meaning of this verse. "Years ago, I worked on a committee to unite two organizations that had been separated for fifty years. For seven long years, we built bridges of hope, trust, and understanding. Then, in an unexpected decision, the organizations came together — but without us. The work was complete, but I felt overlooked and dismissed."

Jesus listened with compassion, his presence like a balm to my spirit. "Jim," he said softly, "love asks us to let go of the need for recognition or validation. Disappointment can steal the joy from your service if you let it. But love transforms even the hardest moments into opportunities to grow."

In that moment, a lightness filled my heart. I realized my disappointment had taken something beautiful and turned it into a burden. Love, I understood, does not dwell on what was lost but celebrates what has been gained.

Jesus placed his hand gently on my shoulder and said, "When disappointment tempts you to focus on what went wrong, remember this prayer: *'Lead me not into temptation, but deliver me from error.'*"

Those words stayed with me, a simple reminder to keep my heart clear. I've learned that when I choose to see the good — to focus on the love present in every outcome — I stay in harmony with what matters most.

Now, when frustration arises, I pause and ask myself: *Can I see this through the eyes of love?* Love doesn't count what is missing; it rejoices in what is complete. It doesn't carry grievances; it carries understanding.

In this way, love becomes our guide, helping us to serve not from obligation but with joy, not for recognition but for the sheer beauty of giving. For love never seeks its own way — it simply gives, and in that giving, it fulfills us all.

~ Corinthians 6 ~

"Love doesn't rejoice in unrighteousness, but rejoices with the truth."

One evening, Jesus spoke to us about the difference between self-righteousness and truth. "It's easy to feel righteous when we believe we are defending justice," he said. "But love doesn't grow from self-righteousness. It finds its strength in truth, and truth often reveals what we'd rather not see."

I shared a personal story to help bring this lesson to life. "In the early 90s, I made a casual remark in class—a joke I thought was harmless. But a woman in the room was upset by what I said, and I realized I had spoken from a place of ignorance. That moment forced me to face a prejudice I hadn't even known I carried."

Feeling shaken, I attended a Goddess Festival in Los Angeles soon after. There, I saw altars honoring the Divine Feminine—symbols of a sacred energy I had overlooked and dismissed. It was like opening a window I didn't know was closed. For the first time, I could see what I had been blind to: a truth that included voices and perspectives beyond my own.

Jesus nodded and said, "Jim, when we cling to our sense of being right, we build walls around our hearts and minds. But truth dissolves those walls. Love doesn't cling to what is comfortable; it invites us to see more clearly."

I thought about the South American natives who mistook the sails of Spanish ships for clouds and welcomed the Conquistadors as gods. Like them, I realized I had misunderstood what I was seeing. My limited perspective had shaped my reality until love—and truth—opened my eyes.

Jesus continued, "Love is about seeking the whole truth, not just holding onto a narrow sense of right and wrong. When we listen with patience and humility, we make space for truth to reveal itself, moment by moment."

That experience changed me. Now, when I feel the pull of righteous anger, I pause. I ask myself: *What am I missing? What truth have I yet to discover?* Love teaches me to listen, to let go of my defenses, and to open my heart to perspectives I had ignored.

In the end, love rejoices not in being right but in finding what is true. It helps us grow, it softens our prejudices, and it leads us to a deeper understanding of one another.

~ Corinthians 7 ~

"Love bears all things, believes all things, hopes all things, endures all things."

Jesus spoke to James, John, and Peter about the strength of love. "Love doesn't give up. It doesn't grow tired or turn away. Love carries us when we are weak and lifts us when we feel alone."

He looked at me, and I felt a memory stir.

"In 1962," I began, "I won a scholarship to a music camp. One afternoon, I sat on a rock and listened to the USC brass choir perform *Fanfare for the Common Man* by Aaron Copland. I was moved to tears. In that moment, I thought, 'I want to do that.'"

Jesus smiled gently and said, "Jim, that moment was love at work — a gift from God, a seed planted in your heart. Love shows up in these moments to guide us, to remind us of what's possible."

Since that day, I've noticed these *"love pivots"* — simple moments that changed my direction. Each one carried me forward, like stepping stones across a river. Even when I didn't understand where I was going, love believed for me, hoped for me, and helped me endure.

Jesus concluded, "When you let love lead, it carries the weight, it believes when you can't, it hopes when things seem lost, and it never gives up. Love is strong enough to see you through anything."

And it has. With every pivot, I've seen love shape my life, quietly and powerfully, into the person I am today. Love truly bears, believes, hopes, and endures all things — always.

~ Corinthians 8 ~

"Love never fails. But where there are prophecies, they will be done away with; where there are various languages, they will cease; where there is knowledge, it will be done away with."

Jesus gathered his disciples and spoke with calm certainty, "Everything in this world will fade — our predictions, our words, our knowledge. But love remains. Love never fails, and it will always guide you to what truly matters."

He turned to Dr. Jim and asked him to share a story.

"Thank you, Jesus," Dr. Jim began. "When my son was in high school, he tried out for the football team despite being small for the sport. He struggled, and when I gently suggested he try something else, he firmly said, 'I'll stick it out, Dad. I'm not a quitter.' He did finish the semester, but in the end, football wasn't for him. Instead, he joined the choir, discovered a love for music, and fell in love with playing the guitar. That passion became his true joy."

Jesus smiled knowingly and said, "Sometimes, what we see as failure is actually the doorway to our greatest joys. Love is sufficient; it always finds the way. When we stop chasing success in others' eyes and follow love, we discover our true path."

I reflected on this, realizing that many of us struggle with what I call *"compare-a-sin"* — the habit of measuring our worth by comparing ourselves to others. We think success, certainty, and approval will complete us. But as Corinthians teaches, even these fade when compared to love.

Jesus looked at us all and said, "When you choose love, the need to compete disappears. Comparison fades away, and you are left with peace."

In my son's story, I saw this truth. Once he let go of the need to prove himself, his love for music blossomed. The struggle ended, and joy took its place. As Jesus reminds us, *'All things come to pass,'* but love remains. It never fails. It carries us home to what is real and lasting.

~ Corinthians 9 ~

"For we know in part, and we prophesy in part."

Jesus sat with John, James, and Peter under a quiet sky. The first stars began to twinkle, like tiny holes in a dark curtain letting heaven's light shine through. His voice was calm and steady, like the sound of water flowing gently over stones.

"My friends," he said, "we don't see everything clearly yet. It's like looking through a foggy window. We catch glimpses of the truth, but God sees the whole picture—clear and bright, like the sky when the clouds disappear."

Dr. Jim then remembered something Dr. Ernest Holmes once taught. He said there's a difference between *faith in God* and the *faith of God*. Holmes explained, *"God is belief, and belief creates our world."*

Jesus nodded and looked at us with kindness in his eyes. "You say you believe in God, but I ask you to go deeper—to have the faith *of* God. True faith doesn't worry or doubt. It's like a mountain. A mountain doesn't try to move or prove itself; it simply *is*. It stands tall, steady, and certain of its place."

Then Jesus turned to me, and his words landed right in my heart. "Jim, can you live your life as one beautiful whole instead of breaking it into little pieces? Life is not meant to be scattered, like toys forgotten in different rooms. It's like a puzzle. Every piece—whether joyful or sad, hard or easy—belongs. Put them together, and you'll see the full picture, a picture made with love."

I thought about this. How often do we split our lives apart, like sorting blocks into different piles—work here, family there, worries in one corner, and faith in another? We think we're in control, but instead, we feel lost and incomplete.

Jesus spoke again, his voice steady and sure. "Let go of the pieces. God's love is complete. It's like the sun—shining for everyone, not in bits and pieces, but as a whole.

You don't need to chase peace. You *are* peace. You don't need to look for love. You *are* love."

In that moment, I understood. Life is not broken or scattered. It is a gift — whole and perfect, even when it feels messy. When we trust God's love and stop dividing our hearts, we find the truth: we are already enough.

From that day, I learned to see life as one great light shining through me. I was no longer just pieces of a person — I was whole, complete, and free, like the stars in the night sky, shining together as part of something greater.

~ Corinthians 10 ~

"But when that which is complete has come, then that which is partial will be done away with."

Jesus explained, "When the fullness of God's presence is known to us, the fragmented pieces we once clung to will fade away. Love fills every gap, bringing harmony and peace."

To illustrate, Dr. Jim shared a story about how we often strive for wealth, clinging to it out of fear of scarcity. "People sometimes hoard their riches, believing they are protecting themselves, but in doing so, they lose sight of the whole picture." Jesus reminded us, *"True wealth is found in giving, in letting good circulate freely, without expectation or attachment."*

He then encouraged us to open our senses to the fullness of life and its blessings. "Imagine looking at a stained-glass window," Jesus said. "If you stand too close, you see only scattered fragments of color—reds, blues, and golds—disconnected and incomplete. But when you step back, the full design is revealed, whole and beautiful. So it is with God's love: we must step back in faith to see its entirety."

Jesus spoke of our senses as tools for understanding this truth. "When we touch, we feel the warmth of another's hand, a reminder of our shared humanity. When we listen, we hear not just noise but the harmony of birdsong or the laughter of a child—echoes of Divine joy. When we look with open eyes, we see the sunlight piercing through clouds, a symbol that even in uncertainty, light is always present."

Then Jesus added, "Giving with an open heart is like tasting the sweetest fruit, its flavor unexpected and fulfilling. It is also the smell of fresh rain on dry earth—renewing and life-giving. When you give without hesitation, you enter the flow of Divine abundance, where love completes all things."

He reminded us of the old adage: *"Don't let the right hand know what the left is doing."* In other words, when we give freely—without strings, without pride—we align with the infinite generosity of God.

Through this, I learned that love and service are the keys to wholeness. Where once there was fear or incompleteness, love replaces every fragment with a sense of unity and purpose. It is in this fullness that we see clearly, not just with our eyes, but with our hearts.

~ Corinthians 11 ~

"When I was a child, I spoke as a child, I felt as a child, I thought as a child. Now that I have become a man, I have put away childish things."

Jesus turned to his disciples and said, "Spiritual maturity means setting aside the judgments, fears, and limited thinking of youth. Like children building sandcastles on the shore, you once viewed life in fleeting pieces, focused only on what was in front of you. But as spiritual adults, you learn to see the whole ocean of existence — deep, vast, and eternal."

I shared with Jesus and the others a story about a conversation I once had with Deepak Chopra regarding his book, *You Are the Universe*. At first, Chopra faced harsh criticism from physicists who opposed his blending of science and spirituality. Like a child stung by rejection, his initial response was anger — a natural reflex of someone defending their creation. But over time, he chose to "put away childish things." He let go of defensiveness and replaced it with patience and kindness, even toward his critics. By embracing the Way of Jesus — love over judgment — he discovered unexpected friendships with those who once stood against him.

Jesus nodded in approval and said, "Anger is the response of a child, quick and impulsive, like storm clouds gathering without rain. But love — love is the calm of a spiritual adult. It is the clear sky after the storm, steady and intentional."

He reminded us of Henry David Thoreau's words: *"to suck out all the marrow of life."* Just as a child sees only the surface of a feast, missing the nourishment within, spiritual adulthood calls us to dig deeper — to find the meaning, purpose, and wholeness beneath life's experiences.

I thought back to my early piano teacher, Eddie. As a boy, I played the notes without feeling, focused only on hitting the right keys. But Eddie taught me to hear the music within the silence, to approach each piece with intention, depth, and authenticity. In the same way, Jesus teaches us to approach life itself as a song — to move beyond surface judgments and embrace the fullness of our spiritual growth.

This lesson of "putting away childish things" is not about losing innocence, but about gaining wisdom. It's the shift from seeing the world as a collection of isolated moments to seeing it as a symphony, whole and complete. To live as spiritual adults is to see beyond the surface, to respond with love instead of reaction, and to embody the Divine intention that calls us home to wholeness.

~ Corinthians 12 ~

"For now we see in a mirror, dimly, but then face to face. Now I know in part, but then I will know fully, even as I am fully known."

Jesus gathered his disciples, his voice calm yet full of promise. "We live in a world of reflections, as though looking into a foggy mirror. What we see now is incomplete, only shadows of the Divine. But a day will come when the fog will clear, and we will see face to face, fully knowing, as God already fully knows us."

To bring this truth to life, I invited Dr. Jim to share a story about reflection, authenticity, and spiritual wholeness.

"Thank you, Jesus," Dr. Jim began, his words gentle but steady. "When I think of authenticity, I imagine a lake at sunrise. At first, its surface is covered in mist, the water unable to reflect the sky in its fullness. That's how our human experience often feels—dim, fragmented, unclear. But as the light of the sun rises higher, the mist begins to lift, and the lake becomes a perfect mirror, reflecting the beauty above it. In the same way, God's love allows the mist of our doubts and fears to clear, revealing the full reflection of our divine potential."

He paused for a moment, then continued, "Jesus often reminded us, 'It is done unto you as you believe.' Life is a mirror. If we believe in scarcity, we see only lack. If we believe in love, we see love reflected everywhere. When I began to understand this truth, I felt my life transform. The fractured pieces of my being began to align, and I could see each part shining with the light of Divine love."

Jesus smiled, adding, "When you release fear and embrace your true nature, you are fully known. To be fully known is to stand in the pure, unconditional love of God—where nothing is hidden, and nothing is broken. It's like coming home to yourself and finding you were whole all along."

In this moment of clarity, we are no longer dim reflections but clear mirrors of Divine truth. The mist disappears, and we see life as it was always meant to be — a union of the human and the holy, face to face with the eternal love of God.

~ Corinthians 13 ~

"And now faith, hope, and love remain, these three; but the greatest of these is love."

Jesus looked at each of us with deep compassion, his voice carrying the weight of timeless truth. "Faith gives us the courage to take the next step, hope points us toward the horizon, but love — the greatest of all — guides us home to God, like a lighthouse drawing weary travelers safely to shore."

To reinforce this truth, I invited Dr. Jim to share a story about a moment that revealed love's enduring power.

"Thank you, Jesus," Dr. Jim began softly. "When my father passed, my siblings and I stood together, hand in hand, a circle of strength in the face of sorrow. Our grief could have torn us apart, but love held us together like roots beneath a mighty tree, unseen but unshakable. In that moment, I understood that love is more than a feeling; it is the force that binds, heals, and sustains us when words fall away."

Jesus nodded, his eyes reflecting understanding. "Love is the foundation of all things. It is the path of forgiveness, the thread of unity, and the heart of true connection."

He then spoke of forgiveness, sharing how it had cleared the way for healing in Patty's life. Through her forgiveness of her father, Patty softened the wall that had stood between them for years. Like sunlight breaking through a storm, forgiveness revealed love's ability to mend what seemed irreparable.

Faith, hope, and love are the sacred tools that guide our lives. But as Jesus reminded us, *love alone remains.* Love transcends time, reaching beyond loss and pain. It is the bridge that unites us with our Creator and the light that brings peace to all who embrace it.

The Way of Jesus calls us to live through love. For in love, we find the fullness of our faith, the realization of our hope, and the very essence of God's presence—eternal, unshaken, and infinite.

Chapter 9
Consider This

The Gift, The Opportunity, The Change

As Jesus concluded his teachings, he looked around at his disciples, his eyes full of warmth and compassion. They gathered close, sensing the significance of the moment. He spoke to them, his voice carrying both gratitude and gentle encouragement.

"I want to thank Dr. Jim Turrell for writing these words," he said. "Inspiring humanity with allegorical wisdom is no small task. These teachings are written to awaken, to inspire, and to challenge each of you to see the sacredness in life."

He paused, as if searching for the right words, then continued, "Albert Einstein once said, 'There are only two ways to live your life. One is as though nothing is a miracle. The other is as though everything is a miracle.' Embrace the latter, for miracles are woven into the fabric of each moment, into the life God has given you."

The disciples nodded, reflecting on his words as he spoke. "Remember, life is a gift and an opportunity for change. Let go of the distractions that pull you from your true purpose. Cherish your unique talents and the gifts you've been given—they are sacred tools for your growth. Let them illuminate your path."

Looking at each of them, Jesus continued, "If you feel lost, pause, breathe, and listen for the voice of God within. Let it remind you that all of life is an invitation to serve, to grow, and to love. Know that every challenge is simply an opportunity, a gentle nudge from the Divine, guiding you toward your highest potential."

He smiled, as if seeing the potential in each of them, and concluded, "Live with faith, as I have shown you. Let your life reflect the truth within you. Allow God's love to shape your journey. Trust in the goodness that flows through all things, and in the unity that binds us to the Divine."

With these final words, the disciples felt a profound peace settle over them. They had been given not just teachings but a way to live — a path illuminated by faith, truth, and the ever-present love of God. Jesus blessed them all and then stood quietly, letting the power of his message fill the silence. And as they embraced the wisdom he had imparted, they knew that the Way he had shown them would live on within their hearts, now and always.